Jewels

for my

GRANDDAUGHTERS

A Gift From My Heart

HELEN FLYNN M.ED. M.S.W.

Jewels for my Granddaughters
A Gift From My Heart

Clareau Press. All rights reserved.
Published by Clareau Press, Sterling, Virginia.

Editor: Christine Frank & Assoc. www.christinefrank.com
Cover and Interior design: Toolbox Creative, www.ToolboxCreative.com

Library of Congress Cataloguing-in-Publications Data
Library of Congress Control Number: 2009932515
Helen Flynn
Jewels for my Granddaughters: A Gift From My Heart
ISBN: 978-0-9841301-0-8
2009

THESE WORDS ARE DIRECTED

TO MY PRECIOUS GRANDDAUGHTERS,

BRIANNE AND SHANNON,

TO GRANDCHILDREN EVERYWHERE,

AND TO THE CHILD'S HEART IN YOU.

Dear Ones,

There is so much I wish I could give you: houses, cars, jewelry, and money; freedom from emotional and physical pain; success, happiness, and a happy ever after. It's probably just as well that I can't give you those things. What I can give you is unconditional love from the bottom of my heart, a legacy of faith in a loving and merciful God, and these little jewels of wisdom that I have gathered along the way.

I love you,
Grandma

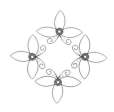

TABLE OF CONTENTS
....

Chapter 1

You Are
Lovable

The love within

sparkles more

brilliantly than

the most precious

diamond.

You Are Lovable
· · · · · · · · · · · · · · · ·

You are loveable. You are loved.
God loves you and I love you.

You are an exquisite creation of God. Not only are
you his creature, you are his beloved child. He wants you
to be happy and to be with him always in heaven. No one
else is exactly like you are. No one else has your unique
gifts. This is why you are loveable. You were created by
Love. If you always remember this, it will affect how you
treat yourself and how you allow others to treat you. If
you truly believe this, you will love and care for your own
body, mind, and spirit. If you truly believe this you will
never allow anyone to mistreat your body, mind, or soul.

Listen to the things you say to yourself. Do
you congratulate yourself when you accomplish

something? Do you recognize your own strengths? Do you encourage yourself? Are you gentle with yourself? Do you believe negative things someone else says to you or about you? If so, why should that be your truth?

We all have faults, yet we must always strive to be all God has created us to be. Humility is knowing our own truth; knowing what is good and what needs empowering.

Do you ever look in the mirror and tell yourself how beautiful you are and that you deserve a good day? Try it. And by the way, don't forget our morning prayer:

Good Morning, Sweet Jesus my Savior,

Good Morning, Sweet Mary, my Mother.

I give you my heart, my soul, and my life.

Keep me from sin and from harm

This day and forever.

Humility is knowing our own truth; knowing what is good and what needs empowering.

Live your day with intent to love and serve God and others.

My mother, your great-grandmother Conway, always taught me to be Christ-like. It took me a long time to understand that that means to be loving. We don't have to go through life with the battle armor on, poised to fight every perceived wrong. Yes, you will be hurt occasionally, sometimes unintentionally, but life is much more manageable if you expect the best from everyone and treat them with your best. As a young adult, I struggled with things (yes, I struggled and made mistakes, just as you will). A dear friend and mentor always suggested that I "do the loving thing." I always go back to those words of wisdom and try to follow them in difficult situations. Time and again they have proven invaluable.

Live your day with intent to love and serve God and others.

CHAPTER 2

BELIEVE IN
Yourself

It is said that there

are forty shades of

green in the Emerald

Isle. May each shade

you see renew your

faith in yourself.

BELIEVE IN YOURSELF

· · · · · · · · · · · · · · · · ·

Whatever you believe you can and can't do,
you are right!

I have had the great joy of watching you both as you learned to walk and talk, swim and ride bikes. You did it in your own way and time.

I often remember watching you both use the piano bench to pull yourselves to a standing position. Little ones naturally work so hard to roll over, stand up, and take a step, while watching adults cheer them on. You don't hear people tell a child, "You'll never succeed with that," or "you'll never walk by yourself." In spite of multiple failures or because of multiple tries, we believe the child will walk and, amazingly, the child never doubts him—or herself.

When does the negative self-talk begin? It usually begins externally by a parent, sibling, or teacher, but we become very skilled at picking up that trend and magnifying it to the nth degree. If you have negative thoughts hiding in your brain, counteract them immediately with positive statements.

You each are developing so many gifts that are uniquely you. Pursue what interests you. Listen to your heart's desire. Your Creator puts those interests and desires within you along with all you need to perfect them if you choose. Don't be afraid to dream "impossible dreams." (That was one of my favorite songs many years ago.) I know now that it is the dreaming along with action that makes dreams possible.

Surround yourself with positive people, people who believe in you. Push out negative thoughts and immediately replace them with positive ones. Be that positive force for others in your life. Be a friend, and you will have true friends.

I know now that it is the dreaming along with action that makes dreams possible.

CHAPTER 3

PAIN AND
Suffering

Seek the blood red

of the ruby

deep within the pain.

Pain And Suffering
· · · · · · · · · · · · · · · · ·

For a very long time I believed that if I was good,
I would avoid pain and suffering. Perhaps that stemmed
from knowing that if I did my work and behaved at
school, I would avoid pain and suffering at home. This
belief was tested and proved painfully correct in the
fourth grade when I got a C in Deportment and a 78 in
Arithmetic. The ensuing pain and suffering led to a
conscious decision to behave and study.

My childish understanding of good and evil,
happiness and sadness, was not seriously challenged
until young adulthood. It was a blessing and a curse,
but certainly all in God's plan.

You have heard me speak of your daddy's
brothers, Michael and Joseph. They were conceived

after your father and both were born prematurely and died shortly after. The miracle and blessing is that both were baptized and are full-fledged saints in heaven, praising God and praying for us. They took the express route and one day we will join them, but we have a lot of work to do first. They were born shortly after *Roe vs Wade* was passed, and I prayed so hard for both of them to survive. Why didn't God answer my prayers? This was a real crisis of faith for me.

In their lifetimes, many people question the goodness of a God that allows death and suffering. I did too. It takes a long time to accept some losses as gifts. I will never truly understand in this life, but I do know that what God sends or allows will be for my ultimate good.

Dear ones, your lives will not be without pain. You have already experienced loss and pain in your lives. Your father's accident and subsequent brain injury have definitely affected your lives. You will ultimately determine how pain and suffering will shape your lives. You cannot always prevent it from happening, but you do have control over how you react to the circumstances of your life. As much as I would like to protect you from it, I cannot and should not. Pain is not all bad. It teaches us compassion, courage, and wisdom. Sometimes it helps us make a major change in the direction of our lives. It may at times seem to be overwhelming, but you will survive to be stronger and more loving. Years ago I taught your father that God always shows us a rainbow when we most need it. It might be a person with just the right word or deed, or a full-fledged arc rainbow, but know He is always there to help you. Look for the rainbows. Look for the miracles.

What God sends or allows
will be for my ultimate good.

CHAPTER 4

YOU AND
Others

May your

relationships with

others reflect the

gentle shadings of

topaz.

You And Others
· · · · · · · · · · · · · · · · ·

Do you ever look at someone and think, "Wow, I wish my life were like hers," or "I wish I had what she has," or "I wish I could be in her shoes."? It's very natural to do that, and that person may be in your life to inspire you to strive for your next level of growth. Remember, though, you see only part of someone else's reality and most of your own. Imagine your life as the full moon and what you see of someone else's life as the quarter moon. There's a vast difference. Likewise, you know your own life story, but see only a snapshot in time of someone else's.

You never know what suffering the angry person might be enduring, or see the insecurities and doubts of the boaster. When someone needs to "put someone down" it is usually coming from their own need to feel better about themselves. The bully could have an abusive or absent father; the mean girl could have a sibling on drugs or a sick mother. We never know someone else's pain. What we can do is pray for the person that hurts us. Believe me, I know it's really hard to do, but a simple "God bless..." will do wonders for them and for you.

Do you remember a song you learned in grade school, "What goes around, comes around, when you give, you receive."? That is a concept that will serve you well throughout your life. In fact, I belong to a networking group whose motto is to give first and share always. It's a great way to do business and to do life.

The fear that somehow there is not enough is the real thief. Think thoughts of abundance. God is our source and love never runs out. I hope that you continue to be generous with your time, your treasure, and your talents. It is hard to think of abundance without thinking of gratitude. I am grateful every day for your existence. Some morning as you struggle to wake up or some night when you can't sleep, start thinking about the things you are grateful for. If something goes wrong, try to find one good thing to say thanks for. Remember the flat tire I had the other day? My whole schedule was turned upside down, but I was so thankful that it happened in the garage and not out in the 90+ degree heat, that I almost didn't mind. If you are really feeling down, start writing a gratitude list. After the first one hundred things, the list gets really good. Can you get to five hundred, one thousand? (Don't forget to be thankful for homework and chores.)

What would you think if a beautiful red rose felt (that is, pretending a rose can feel) that it wasn't as lovely, graceful, talented, and smart as an orchid? What if a gorgeous exotic rare orchid were sad that it didn't have the petals, long stem, or thorns of a rose? You can guess I am talking about you. You each are totally and uniquely you, with all your beautiful characteristics. Be the rose and be proud. Be the orchid and be proud. No one is exactly like you. No one else before or to come will be exactly like you. No one has been made to fulfill your unique role in this life. You have within you all the gifts you need to become whatever your heart desires. Take the gifts you have and nurture them. If something is difficult and you love it, work hard and it will come. Let your light shine! Let your gift spread and your soul take flight!

Give first and share always

CHAPTER 5

Addictions

*May you never
experience the black
onyx of addiction.*

Addictions

. . . .

Another crisis in my life, which I now see as one of my greatest blessings, developed gradually when I was twenty to thirty years old. Along with other Irish ancestors, I became an alcoholic. That was certainly not on my list of things to be when I grew up! I clearly remember the moment when alcohol met a huge need in me. It was after an opera performance where I was celebrating a great success and trying to soothe deep personal pain. The alcohol worked for both and became my ally through the next period of my life. Thanks to a wonderful doctor—one you know well, Dr. Marc Plescia—I got the help I needed in a treatment center and learned invaluable life lessons in 12-step programs. Gradually my faith was renewed and deepened as I matured as a recovering person.

The wisdom learned these last 20+ years has brought security, joy, peace, contentment, and a foundation for living I would never have known. What seemed to be the lowest point of my life became one of the greatest blessings in my life.

Please know that a predisposition for addiction is in your genetic makeup. If you choose to drink, please be very careful. If you ever need pain medication, please be cautious. If someone offers you a substance for kicks, know that the consequences can be disastrous. Finally, please look out for each other. Do not remain silent if someone you love is in difficulty.

I hope you will always have compassion and empathy for those suffering from the disease of addiction or from mental illness. It was my great privilege to serve many suffering people as a substance abuse counselor and social worker. It is a tremendous joy to walk beside someone on the road to recovery. I hope you will seek help if you need it, and give support to any suffering people that cross your path. I believe people are put in our lives to help us or for us to help them.

I believe people are put in
our lives to help us or for us
to help them.

CHAPTER 6

Forgiveness

May you always

know the cooling

amethyst touch of

forgiveness.

Forgiveness

· · · · · · · · · · · · · · · ·

Do you remember being taught that "please" and "thank you" are magic words? "I love you" is generally accepted as valuable, but "I'm sorry" may be the least used and most difficult to say. As children, you knew how important the words were. Often a "Say you're sorry!" would echo loudly in the back seat of my car. Parents and grandparents urge reluctant warriors to say them, even if without heart. Somehow even the most insincere "sorry" helps. Why is it that saying those words feels like we are slicing off a piece of ourselves? Yet, saying a sincere and simple "I'm sorry" can defuse a major argument. Must we always be right? Does it really matter?

Sometimes an altercation can become so complex: both parties owe the other a sincere apology, and it becomes a power struggle not to "give in" first. However, expressing sorrow and acknowledging one's own fault can be very empowering. Parents are often so afraid of losing status in their children's eyes that they don't dare apologize. But in fact, the opposite is true. What a valuable group of lessons a parent or teacher gives when they apologize for their words, tone, or actions.

Because you are human and alive it is inevitable that you will hurt others and be hurt. Learn to cherish the gift of forgiveness and give it freely, whether you receive it in the end or not. Seek it sooner rather than later from those you hurt. You will not go through life without being hurt, by both people who love you and people who hate you. Without forgiveness, the anger you hold will poison your heart. It doesn't make an injustice right and it doesn't punish the person who hurts you; it only destroys the love and light within you.

Sometimes we have to pray for the grace to forgive. Sometimes we may ask God to bless a particular person in spite of what we may feel. Sometimes it takes time to be able to forgive, so we pray to become ready. Our model is Christ and his Mother who forgave his murderers and who daily forgives us. We can do no less.

Sometimes we have to pray
for the grace to forgive.

Chapter 7

Old Messages

Turn the dullness

of old messages

into striking

sapphire truths.

OLD MESSAGES
· · · · · · · · · · · · · · · ·

    Beliefs about ourselves picked up in childhood can have long-lasting effects if we let them. When I was in second grade I got the message that I wasn't very good in math. I'm not really sure where that came from. I don't remember ever liking math, but that may be because I didn't think I was good at it. I carried that belief through college where statistics became my nemesis. Finally in graduate school I determined that I was going to conquer this belief once and for all—and did—with an A in Tests and Measurements. Several years later I bit the bullet and started my master's in Social Work, knowing there would be three courses in Statistics at the end of the program. This was enough to deter me from starting, but I refused to let that happen. I worked hard, asked for help when I needed it, and succeeded. It's amazing to me how a belief from childhood, even one with no validity, can impact your whole life. My math fears had even kept me from pursuing a career in real estate twenty years earlier.

Do you have any beliefs you carry from when you were younger? I have known adults of all ages who, because of something someone said, believed themselves to be fat, stupid, lazy, unwanted, incompetent, not good enough, and on and on. If you have any such negative thoughts, run, don't walk, for a pencil and write a contrary positive statement as many times as it takes to erase that negative thought. If you still struggle, see a therapist and be free of it.

Have you ever made a mistake or gotten into trouble and felt like your life or your happiness was over; that no one would ever speak to you or love you again? That has got to be one of the worst feelings in the world. One of the benefits of living a few decades is realizing that we all make lots of mistakes, that we survive, we learn and grow, and we are still loved. The important thing is to not stay in the mistake, keep repeating it, or condemn ourselves forever because of it. We all make mistakes—presidents, CEOs, celebrities, doctors, teachers, parents, and children—because we are human. It is crucial that we forgive ourselves, change what we must, make amends, and go forward.

I used to use the image of a burned-out forest with my recovering clients. Can you imagine standing in a burned-out forest with death and destruction all around you? If you turn 180 degrees, though, you see the clearing where the devastation has not struck, where the sun is shining. Put one foot in front of the other and walk toward it. Don't stay focused on the damage; focus on where there is light and hope. It is always there if you seek it. No matter how bad you may believe your life and circumstances to be, they can be rebuilt one day at a time. I was blessed to see that happen over and over in the lives of people recovering from addiction, abuse, illness, and loss. If you find some day you need help, by all means, get it. I have seen many beautiful people paralyzed by events in their past. Don't get old blaming your past for your unfortunate present. It is in your power to make positive choices for yourself today.

*Don't stay focused on the
damage; focus on where
there is light and hope.*

CHAPTER 8

Death

Sadness and beauty

coexist in the opal

and in the soul.

DEATH

· · · · · · · · · · · · · · · · ·

    Your first experience with death was when your great-grandfather died. You were just four and five years old and he was almost ninety. You were lucky to have spent some wonderful time with him. He loved you so much and you naturally bonded with him, as children do with the elderly. I love to look back over pictures of you with him and the love and joy in all of your eyes. At his wake we allowed you to be fully present and what gracious, loving young ladies you were. I'm sure Great-Grandpa was smiling down when he saw your reaction to the Knights of Columbus in full regalia and swords and especially when your young voices spoke the Hail Mary's of the Rosary.

    Death is such a difficult concept for a child. Tears came often as you missed Great-Grandpa. It is difficult for all of us to feel that sadness and to move through it to cherishing the memories in our hearts. All the important people in your life will always hold a place in your heart. And, yes, your hearts are big enough to hold them all.

What do you do when you lose someone you love dearly? You grieve, you cry, you get angry, you pretend it didn't happen, and then you do it all over, again and again. Eventually the tears start healing, the anger fades, and good memories and even laughter begin to dominate. The waves of grief engulf you less often and less intensely. There is no shortcut through grief. If you bury it, it will emerge later with fresh pain. Allow yourself to feel it and shed as many tears as you need. You might need to put some time boundaries on your grieving sessions, like thirty minutes, then go on to the business at hand. You may need a support group or therapist if you are drowning in the grief over a period of time. No one can tell you how long to grieve or how to grieve. Your grief will be unique to you. Know, however, that you will heal. You will come to a place of acceptance where you will cherish the memory of the person lost, and go forward a stronger person with a beautiful memory in your heart.

No one can tell you how long

to grieve or how to grieve.

CHAPTER 9

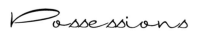

Possessions

Pearls and

possessions can be

associated with tears

and luminescence.

POSSESSIONS

· · · · · · · · · · · · · · · · ·

You know how much I love taking you on shopping sprees and seeing your faces light up when I say "yes" to an outfit or toy or whatever. It is so hard to say "no" to you about anything, but sometimes I have to. It is such fun for me to surprise you at birthdays and Christmas. So far you both appreciate what you have and are very quick to give to anyone who asks. I pray you keep this trait of generosity.

There will always be people who have more of whatever than you. If that small twinge of jealousy appears, focus on what you do have and reach out to someone else who is hurting. Know that things are not the source of happiness. Have you noticed that the day after or even the hour after shopping, the thrill is gone? Have you also noticed how tempting it is to get one more thing?

Financial responsibility is something I hope you will learn more and more as you go through your teens. When you earned money performing, I was so proud that you saved 50 percent, spent 25 percent, and gave 25 percent to charity. I think you felt pretty good, too. As you go forward, try for an 80-10-10 split. Having specific short-term and long-term goals will help too. I'm always amused at your restraint when I suggest you use your own money for a purchase. Knowing you have even a little money set aside in the bank gives you the confidence that if something really important, like your choir trip, comes up, you can pay your own way.

You've seen news stories of victims of hurricanes and fires who lose their homes and everything in them. Always act on your instinct to reach out and help, but know that the building and the things inside can be gone in an instant. Who you are, who you love, what you do, what you feel, your memories, and the people who love you are what matter. Money and things are neither good nor evil. What matters is what you do with them.

Know that things are not the source of happiness.

CHAPTER 10

A
Celebration

Take time to see

the turquoise calm

waters in the events

in your life.

A Celebration

· · · · · · · · · · · · · · · ·

You girls have always loved it when relatives visit
or we visit them. This year's Thanksgiving reunion in
Rochester was unexpected and memorable. Almost all
of the Flynn clan was together. Holding hands while
your grandfather said the Blessing and asked us to
share what we are grateful for was a priceless moment.
As one of the "older" generation, I couldn't help but
think of two sets of great-grandparents of yours who
would be very proud to see you growing into lovely, kind
young ladies. They cooked many turkeys and celebrated
many occasions, teaching us the importance of family
and thanks-giving. I know that my parents and your
grandfather's parents were with us in spirit. Your
uncles, Michael and Joseph, were with us in spirit, too.
Having followed our usual Rochester-visit tradition

of visiting cemeteries, they were all in the forefront of our minds. I think it was especially so for your father who had not visited in some years. He was flooded with memories and insights as he stood at the graves of his beloved grandparents and the brothers he never knew.

In the family circle, he was one of four cousins in two generations that we realized were miracles to be alive. All had miraculously survived accidents that nearly cost them their lives. The two older cousins, now parents, held their children's hands a little tighter on that thought.

Typical of Irish families, we come together for wakes and funerals, but how wonderful it was to come together in joy to celebrate family and blessings. No family is without its misunderstandings, heartaches, tragedies, and pain, but for that moment the past remained past and the future was yet to come. That moment was a graced moment. In that present was tremendous joy, acceptance, and hope. Some of the younger ones got into trouble, a couple got hurt, there were a few tears, but most of all, memories were made to be cherished by future generations.

On this trip we stayed in my parents' home. Great-Grandpa's presence is very much there, with pictures of you with him in several places. His second wife, Dorothy, has been a true great-grandmother to you and was thrilled to have you visit. Her little bird will never be the same. It's probably still looking for the two creatures that chased it all over the house. I'm glad you got to meet Dorothy's older sister, Helen. Even at ninety-four, she's ready to take on the world. Their sister, Janet, is always so good to you, too. You were wishing for gingerbread houses and what did she leave for you? They are a wonderful example of the bond sisters can have throughout their lives. I hope you will have the same.

It was such a treat to drive through neighborhoods long familiar to me and hear you point out houses you liked. The pink stucco with turrets was the winner, I think. I loved showing you the outside of the house I grew up in, my elementary school, and even the church Grandpa and I were married in. I love sharing the beautiful memories in my life with you. It was great fun to visit the Strong Museum of Play and see you fling off teen constraints and just have fun. That will become a destination spot on future trips. To top it all off, there was snow! Although we didn't get to go sledding, you had a blast playing in the big backyard.

This was a totally different Thanksgiving for you. I know how much you like to keep traditions, but sometimes it is good to break them, change them, or develop entirely new ones. The important thing is to realize that people are the root of the celebration, and the tradition must serve to celebrate the family.

Come together in joy to celebrate family and blessings.

CHAPTER 11

YOUR
Tapestry

*Create your one-of-
a-kind life tapestry
on a rich amber
background.*

Your Tapestry

· · · · · · · · · · · · · · · ·

You are both very artistic and express
yourselves in many different mediums. Try to think
of your lives as a beautiful tapestry or mosaic. If you
look at the underside of needlework, it appears to
be random and even messy, but on the other side,
a beautiful picture or design emerges. I've always
thought it is very like our lives. From where we
stand at any given moment, our lives can look pretty
random and even messy, but eventually we come
to see patterns. If you look at one small section of
a mosaic, you may see only black or colorless tiles.
Each event and each person in our lives creates
a new design and color, so that eventually we can
see dark or dull periods interspersed with bright,
dynamic sections. I wonder how you would draw the

tapestry of your lives so far? As you add new threads and new designs, I hope you will add a few of the little jewels I give to you from my heart.

Try to think of your lives as a
beautiful tapestry or mosaic.

REALTOR®, COACH, AUTHOR

Helen Flynn has experienced a multi-faceted career that includes being an educator, social worker, psychotherapist, professional harpist, coach, speaker, writer and Realtor®. Today she successfully blends her interests and skills in her real estate business, assisting buyers and sellers with a major life change, and in her coaching of individuals and groups. She speaks on a variety of topics related to leadership, self-determination, personal responsibility, and interpersonal relationships.

HELEN FLYNN MED., MSW, CLC
Realtor®, Certified Coach, Founder
and President of CLAREAU COACHING:
www.ClareauCoaching.com

Helen's belief in continuing education and personal growth give her a foundation of both knowledge and experience that she shares with others. Her innate ability to listen compassionately and speak with wisdom and gentleness, as well as her peacefulness has allowed her to positively impact many lives.

Helen received her Bachelor of Music degree from the Eastman School of Music, a Master's degree in Educational Administration from the University of Rochester, and a Master of Social Work from Virginia Commonwealth University. She belongs to the National and Virginia Association of Realtors, the International Coaching Federation, the International Speakers Network, eWomen Network, and local chambers of commerce and networking groups. She is an agent with Weichert Realtors in Great Falls, Virginia, and founded her coaching company, Clareau Coaching in 2006.

Being Grandma to two beautiful girls, Brianne and Shannon, being married to her high school sweetheart, Leo, and being deeply devoted to the God of her understanding are the roots of her joy.

Breinigsville, PA USA
01 November 2009
226815BV00001B/4/P

9 780984 130108